> GLOBAL ISSUES

# HUMAN TRAFFICKING

**Kaye Stearman**

WAYLAND

First published in 2008 by Wayland

Wayland
338 Euston Road
London NW1 3BH

Wayland Australia
Level 17/207 Kent Street
Sydney NSW 2000

Senior Editor: Claire Shanahan
Designer: Phipps Design
Photo Researcher: Kath Kollberg
Proofreader and Indexer: Jo Kemp

British Library Cataloguing in Publication Data
Stearman, Kaye
Human trafficking. - (Global issues)
1. Human trafficking - Juvenile literature
2. Human smuggling - Juvenile literature
I. Title
364.1'5

ISBN 978 0 7502 5435 9

African Pictures: Djibril Sy/Panapress p40. Corbis: Danny Lehman p14, Carlos Barria/Reuters p15,
J.Ragel/EFE/epa p16, Mimi Mollica p22, Ho/ Reuters p26, Jeffrey L. Rotman p32, Envision p38,
Francoise de Mulder p39. Getty Images p5, p6, p7, p8, p10, Peter Busomoke/Afp p12,
Jay Directo/Afp p21, p44. Mary Evans Picture Library: p9. NI Syndication: p43. Pa Photos:
AP Photo/Chris Brandis p18. Reuters: Noel Kokou Tadegnon FOR/TZ p29, SA/FY/AA p36.
Rex Features: Roger-Viollet p4, Lena Kara p13, Dave Gatley p20, p25, Jonathan Hordle p33,
Denis Cameron p23, Kristy-Anne Glubish / Design Pics Inc p34, Everett Collection p42.

Printed in China

Wayland is a division of Hachette Children's Books,
an Hachette Livre UK company.
www.hachettelivre.co.uk

# Contents

# Chapter 1

# What is Human Trafficking?

Human trafficking is a form of slavery. In simple terms, it is the buying, selling and transporting of human beings, for exploitation and abuse. It may take place within a country but increasingly it involves crossing international borders, by land, sea and air.

The United Nations (UN), formed in 1945, defines 'trafficking in persons' as, 'the recruitment, transportation, transfer, harbouring or receipt of persons, by means of the threat or use of force or other forms of coercion, of abduction, of fraud, of deception…for the purpose of exploitation.'

There are several types of trafficking, including:

**Traditional slavery** – ownership of other human beings, so that they are treated as property that can be bought, sold, inherited or given to others. Although slavery has been officially abolished worldwide, it still exists in some countries. A slave is under the total control of their owner and is expected to work without payment.

*In the 19th century the economy of the American south was dependent on slave labourers working in the cotton fields.*

**People smuggling** – involves transporting people across international borders, in an illegal or clandestine way. While deceit, fraud and exploitation may be used by the smugglers, those being smuggled are doing so on a voluntary basis, because they seek work or want to escape from war or political persecution. Once their journey is finished, they are no longer bound to the smugglers.

**Human trafficking** – involves transporting people within a country or across international borders in an illegal or clandestine way, in order to exploit them through work or by selling their services. Unlike smuggling, those being trafficked do not do this on a voluntary basis. Either they are taken against their will, do not realise what is involved or are deliberately misled or deceived. For example, they may be promised a good job or an education, but then find themselves working in the sex industry or as a domestic servant. In effect, they have become slaves.

**Child labour** – most child labour occurs in poor countries and usually takes place in or close to home, on farms or in small workshops. According to the United Nations Children's Fund (UNICEF), 250 million children aged 5 to 17 are working as child labourers. However, some children are bought and sold as slaves, abducted or smuggled across borders. The United Nations says that children cannot give proper consent, and any type of recruitment, transportation, transfer, harbouring or receipt of children for exploitation is a form of trafficking.

*A commemoration and an apology. Queen Elizabeth is joined by religious leaders at a service at Westminister Abbey in March 2007 to mark the bicentenary of the Abolition of the Slave Trade Act.*

However, the line between these categories is often quite a thin one. What might start out as a voluntary act can easily become human trafficking, especially when it involves crossing international borders and criminal gangs.

## Invisible people

Given the fact that trafficking is an illegal and hidden activity, it is not surprising that there are no reliable statistics.

The United Nations Office on Drugs and Crime (UNODC) estimates that at any one time 2.5 million people are victims of trafficking. In 2005, a report by the US State Department estimated that between 600,000 and 800,000 people each year were trafficked across international borders.

However, many people believe that the real numbers are much higher. The International Labour Organisation (ILO) estimates there are 12.3 million victims,

*Fear and regret on the face of young girl in Cambodia. She was rescued from captivity in a brothel by the Cambodian Women's Crisis Centre.*

while the campaigning group Free the Slaves says there are 27 million people worldwide, although this includes traditional slavery.

## The victims

UNODC estimates that 80 per cent of trafficked people are women and children (under 18 years of age), with men making up the remaining 20 per cent. Others dispute this, saying that men make up a higher proportion but are less visible. In fact, almost all trafficked people are invisible. Women and children are mainly involved in the sex trade or in domestic work, while men are more likely to work as labourers.

UNODC has recorded trafficking taking place in 137 countries. This includes origin countries (countries where people are trafficked from) and destination countries (countries where people are trafficked to). Some countries are both origin and destination countries. The greatest numbers of trafficking victims are recorded as coming from Thailand, China, Nigeria, Albania, Bulgaria, Belarus, Moldova and Ukraine. Thailand was also a destination country, as were Japan, Israel, Belgium, the Netherlands, Germany, Italy, Turkey, the UK and the USA.

## The traffickers

Human trafficking is an unlawful activity, carried out by criminal gangs, who are highly organised and very violent against each other and their victims.

The reason why criminals are involved is very simple. Trafficking is both illegal and highly profitable. According to UNODC, human trafficking is the third largest moneymaker for criminals, after drugs and weapons. In some ways, it can be more profitable. Drugs and weapons can be sold only once, but a slave can be sold over and over again. UNODC estimates total profits from trafficking at US$32 billion, with US$10 billion from the initial sale of people and the remainder from selling the goods or services they provide.

> QUOTE >
>
> 'Human trafficking is a crime that strips people of their rights, exploits people's dreams of a better future, robs people of their dignity. It can cause physical and psychological damage. It can even kill.'
>
> UN Secretary-General **Ban Ki-moon**, speaking at premiere of the film *Trade* in New York, USA, 19 September 2007.

*A rare case of traffickers being caught, prosecuted and punished. Three Albanian men in court in Tirana, Albania, in March 2004, accused of involvement in the kidnap of a four-year-old girl.*

# Chapter 2

# The History of Human Trafficking

Human trafficking is not a new practice – it is as old as recorded history. Trafficking in human beings took place under the Egyptian pharaohs 4,000 years ago and in the empire of the Hittites in Mesopotamia, in ancient Greece and in the Roman Empire, where 20 per cent of the population may have been slaves. Trafficking often took place in the aftermath of war when prisoners of war and conquered peoples were sold into slavery. Many were transported across the Mediterranean to build the great monuments of Rome, toil in the fields or serve in the villas of the Roman elite.

Trafficking continued in many parts of the world for the next 2,000 years. As longer land and sea routes opened up, traffickers tapped new supplies of human beings. The most notorious was the development of the Transatlantic slave trade, transporting slaves from Africa to North and South America and the Caribbean.

## The transatlantic slave trade

Slavery and trafficking were not new in Africa. They had existed before European expansion, and Arab traffickers had developed slave markets along the east African coast. The Transatlantic slave trade was different in its reach, extent and timespan.

*1835: Slaves aboard a slave ship are shackled before being placed in the hold for the long dangerous voyage across the Atlantic to the Americas.*

| 1792 Denmark passes law against slavery >>> | 1802 Denmark bans trading in slaves >>> | 1807 UK bans slave trade in British colonies >>> | 1809 USA bans citizens from international slave trade >>> |
|---|---|---|---|

The trade started with the exploration of Africa, Asia and the Americas by sailors from the Portuguese and Spanish empires with their improved ships and navigation devices. Invasion and conquest soon followed. Both empires wanted slave labour to sow and harvest profitable crops in the newly conquered Americas, and so began to buy and transport slaves from Africa across the Atlantic. In the following centuries, they were joined by slavers from France, Britain, the Netherlands and other nations. The trade continued for four centuries with an estimated total of 12 million Africans enslaved and trafficked, although many died on the voyage or soon after arrival.

The Transatlantic slave trade reached its height in the 18th century. By this stage, there were political movements in several countries to end slavery, but this was a minority position and it took years to change the situation. Denmark led the way, passing a law against slavery in 1792. Britain banned the slave trade in

*Until 1832, the British parliament was dominated by wealthy landowners, some of whom were also slave owners or investors in the slave trade. For twenty years, they opposed William Wilberforce's attempts to end the slave trade.*

the British Empire in 1807, and the USA banned the import of slaves in 1808. However, slavery itself was abolished in the British Empire only in 1833 (and continued for several years after this) and in the USA during the Civil War, in 1863. The last country to act was Brazil, which freed all slaves in 1888.

QUOTE >

'The slave trade was "profoundly shameful"…we condemn its existence utterly and praise those who fought for its abolition'.

**Tony Blair,** former UK Prime Minister, 27 November 2006.

**1820** Spain bans slave trade in Spanish colonies (except Cuba) >>>

**1833** Slavery banned in British territories >>>

**1848** France bans slavery and frees slaves >>>

**1853** Brazil bans slave trade >>>

**1888** Brazil frees slaves >>>

# Case Study: William Wilberforce, anti-slavery campaigner

In 2007, the UK marked the two hundredth anniversary of the abolition of the slave trade. There were marches, religious services, parliamentary debates, films, concerts, exhibitions – even a new International Slavery Museum in Liverpool, one of the main slave trade ports.

Media attention focused on the role of William Wilberforce (1759–1833), whose bill abolishing the slave trade passed through Parliament on 25 March 1807. Wilberforce was elected as Member of Parliament for the city of Hull when he was only 21. He collected evidence of the cruelty of the slave trade, travelled widely and spoke at hundreds of meetings. He gathered almost 400,000 signatures on a petition demanding an end to the slave trade. However, his attempts to abolish the slave trade through Parliament were defeated by slave owners and their supporters for 20 years.

Critics said that there was too much attention on the role of Wilberforce, rather than other campaigners, such as Thomas Clarkson or Olaudah Equianio, who was a former slave. They pointed out that slavery had been supported by British institutions, including the ruling classes, the law and the church. This was hardly a heritage to celebrate.

Furthermore, they felt that the legacy of the slave trade lingered in modern Britain. Black and other ethnic minorities were still treated less fairly than white people. Discrimination, prejudice and violence still existed. Campaigners called for an official government apology and for reparations to be paid to the descendants of slaves.

*William Wilberforce, the leading parliamentary campaigner against the slave trade. His bill to abolish the slave trade in Britain and its colonies finally passed on 25 March 1807.*

| **1780** William Wilberforce elected as MP for Hull >>> | **1787** Abolition Committee founded by anti-slavery activists >>> | **1789** Wilberforce introduces first parliamentary bill to abolish slave trade >>> |
|---|---|---|

# WHAT THE WORLD THINKS...

These are two different news stories commenting on William Wilberforce and his legacy. Compare and contrast the viewpoints and see if you can find any more newspaper reports or other media discussing him and his impact on slavery.

**'Arthur: Give back to slave's children',
Daily Nation,
27 March 2007**

'Prime Minister Arthur Owen wants those who were at the heart of the Transatlantic Slave Trade (Britain) to address the issue of reparation to the descendants of former slaves.

While praising the efforts of William Wilberforce 200 years ago in the fight against slavery, he told those in the Holy Trinity Church in Hull, England, on Sunday that there was still unfinished business that must be dealt with. He was delivering the 2007 Wilberforce Lecture.'

*Daily Nation is a newspaper in Barbados.*

**Len Tingle,
*BBC News* website
8 December 2006**

'...March 2007 will mark the 200th anniversary of Parliament voting in favour of the "Abolition of the Slave Trade" Act, a vote that changed the face of world history – and the campaign to end slavery was led by local MP William Wilberforce...

A huge programme of events has been set up in Hull, culminating on 25 March 2007, when the Prime Minister of Barbados, Owen Arthur, visits Hull to open the upgraded Wilberforce Museum, and deliver the Wilberforce Lecture on freedom and democracy. Hull City Council is organising a year of commemoration, both to make people aware of the achievements of Wilberforce and to bring home the message that slavery is still a very real issue in various parts of the world.'

*Les Tingle is the Political Editor for BBC Yorkshire and Lincolnshire.*

**1807** Parliament votes to abolish slave trade in British colonies >>> | **1825** Wilberforce retires as MP >>> | **1833** Wilberforce dies two days after slavery abolished in British colonies >>>

**11**

## Slavery exists today

Slavery still exists today. The most common form, involving the largest numbers, is child labour. The International Labour Organisation (ILO) says that worldwide there are 250 million children aged between 5 and 17 who are full-time workers, with 179 million doing jobs that are difficult and dangerous. Most live in Asia, mainly in India, Pakistan and Bangladesh. Many children work close to their families, on farms or in small workshops, but a significant number work away from home, as labourers or domestic servants.

Some children are trafficked as bonded labourers. A bonded labourer is someone who has borrowed money from an employer and agrees to work to pay off the debt. Often a child is bonded to repay a parent's debt, working long hours far from home, unable to escape.

Sometimes children are trafficked across countries. The UN Children's Fund (UNICEF), has recorded a flourishing traffic in children in west Africa, an area affected by poverty and wars. Ships crammed with children have been found on the same African coastline as the original Transatllantic slave trade. Many end up as domestic servants in oil-rich Gabon.

## The victims of war

Wars and conflicts have promoted their own forms of slavery. Over a period of 20 years, thousands of children have been abducted from villages in northern Uganda by a rebel army. Once captured, the boys are forced to fight and the girls to become servants and `girlfriends' of soldiers. They become brutalised by their captors and even those who escape are

*The victims of war. Some of the thousands of children made refugees by the brutality of a rebel army in northern Uganda. Many children have been kidnapped and enslaved by the rebels.*

| According to UNICEF: >>> | 2 million children have been killed by conflict over the last decade >>> | 6 million children have been made homeless >>> | 12 million children have been injured or disabled >>> |
| --- | --- | --- | --- |

*Although slavery has been formally abolished in Mauritania, a desert country in western Africa, many people continue to live as slaves, like these children of slaves who work for their food and lodging.*

afraid to return to their families in fear and shame at what they have done.

There are similar stories from other countries. In Sudan, thousands of people were captured during the war in the south and taken as slaves to government controlled areas. With the end of the war in 2005, many slaves were freed under a United Nations sponsored programme and returned to their homes. Although they find life very hard in their devastated villages, they still consider themselves better off than the thousands who remain as slaves as in the north.

QUOTE >

'Slavery is a booming international trade, less obvious than two hundred years ago for sure, but all around us. Perhaps we simply prefer to close our eyes to it, as many law abiding citizens buy the products and the services produced on the cheap by slaves.'

**Antonio Maria Costa**, Executive Director at UNDOC, 25 March 2007 at the Launch of the Global Initiative to Fight Human Trafficking (UN-GIFT), 26 March 2007.

 At least 300,000 child soldiers operate in 30 different conflicts >>>

# Chapter 3

# Porous Borders – People Smuggling

## A world on the move

Every year millions of people cross international borders in search of work, a practice that has increased with improved transport and communications. While wealthy countries often welcome skilled immigrants, their doors are closed to most people from the poorest countries.

As a result many people turn to people smugglers, paying large sums of money to travel clandestinely across borders. Once they reach their destination, they hope to find work, to save and to send money home to their families.

People smuggling is not new. For the past century, millions of immigrants from Mexico and central America have travelled to the USA. Some come legally, but many pay coyotes or gang members to guide them across the long US border. The most common method is smuggling groups through gaps in the border, trying to elude the US border patrols, but some coyotes transport people in trucks or cars or tunnel under the border fence.

The practice is a result of both 'pull' and 'push' factors. On the one hand, the USA

*Two young Mexican men wait amid the heat and dust for the chance to cross the US border, just as many thousands do each year.*

| | 1988 | 1993 | 2000 |
|---|---|---|---|
| **Research by the University of Houston shows hundreds of deaths each year of immigrants crossing from Mexico to the USA. Estimates include:** >>> | 255 deaths >>> | 180 deaths >>> | 370 deaths >>> |

has a vibrant economy with a huge demand for labour; on the other, the countries to the south face increasing poverty. Although illegal immigrants are frequently deported to their home countries, many more arrive.

A more recent development is people smuggling from Asia and Africa to Europe. Most people come by land, smuggled in cars or lorries across the many European borders. Many Africans face a long land journey across the Sahara desert, then a sea journey across the Mediterranean.

## Smuggling routes

As one route closes, so other routes open. In the 1990s, most migrants crossed the US border in California. When border defences were strengthened there, the focus shifted to Texas and then to Arizona. The result was that migrants found themselves lost or abandoned in hostile desert country, without maps or contacts, food or water. Others were killed by gang members, vigilantes or border guards. According to the US Border Patrol, almost 2,500 people died crossing the border in the years 1998–2005. The true numbers are likely to be higher.

Similarly, routes from Africa to Europe have changed. Many boats still cross from north Africa, heading for Italy or Spain. The shortest crossing is the narrow strait from Morocco to Spain. When patrols from both countries cracked down on this route, migrants started to use a longer and even more dangerous route, sailing from Mauritania, Senegal, Gambia and Cape

Verde to Spain's Canary Islands. Up to 10,000 Africans are believed to have drowned attempting to reach Europe in the years from 2003 to 2005.

Governments in north Africa and in Europe are now taking tougher action to deter migrants, and numbers attempting the sea crossing seem to be dropping. However, dangers – and casualties – remain high.

*Young men travel on a cargo train to the border city of Nuevo Laredo in Mexico. Thousands of would-be immigrants travel this route, not just from Mexico but from the Central American countries further south.*

## Is people smuggling human trafficking?

Some people describe people smuggling as a new form of slavery, especially in the type of conditions that people endure, crammed into tiny boats or in lorries. However, unlike slavery, people smuggling is nearly always undertaken on a voluntary basis.

*They have reached Europe at last, but these would-be immigrants are lucky to have escaped with their lives after crossing the Strait of Gibraltar from Morocco to Spain.*

Nevertheless, like other forms of human trafficking, people smuggling routinely involves deceit, fraud and exploitation. Many migrants are cheated or treated badly, finding themselves dumped in a

| | |
|---|---|
| **Jan 2002–July 2003** 742 would-be immigrants documented as dying trying to enter EU >>> | **2005** Dutch NGO United claim that 6,336 would-be immigrants died between 1993 and 2005 while crossing from north Africa to Europe >>> |

strange country or abandoned at sea. Many people do not make it, some lose their lives.

People smuggling is controlled by criminal gangs, who are also often involved with the drug trade or money laundering. Sometimes these go hand in hand, as do drug smuggling and people smuggling on the US-Mexican border. People-smuggling gangs are secretive and violent, and are rarely caught or punished. Smugglers are unlikely to have contact with people before or after they have arrived in their destination country.

## The cost of smuggling

Coyotes on the US-Mexican border demand large fees for their services. As the US government strengthens its borders, making the crossing harder and more dangerous, so the coyotes' fees rise. In 2003, the average cost of a border crossing was between US$500 and US$1,000, but, by 2006, it had risen to between US$2,500 and US$3,000. On the sea routes from Africa to Europe, fees can be 1,000 to 2,000 euros or more. Added to this are the costs of the land journey to the coast, across the harsh Sahara desert, plus visa costs and bribes to corrupt officials. Those who can afford air fares can travel in greater comfort, but also face the risk of being turned back by immigration officers.

Why do people pay such large sums? Although they come from poor countries, they tend not to be the poorest people. They see images of Western affluence on

> **QUOTE >**
>
> 'As I was lounging by my holiday pool, I suffered a nasty jolt by reading in the newspaper that 14 bodies had been found floating in the sea between Tunisia and Sicily – victims of an iniquitous traffic in illegal immigrants between north Africa and Italy. Their identities are unknown, as is the manner in which they died…The victims could have been pushed out to sea in some kind of dinghy that then sank; or they simply could have been thrown overboard.'
>
> **Alexander Chancellor**, columnist, *Guardian*, 17 August 2007.

television and in advertisements. Some already have relatives abroad and have access to some funds, for example by selling land or borrowing from family members. Some are refugees seeking asylum from wars and political persecution. But all believe that migration will offer them a chance of a better life for themselves and their families, and so are prepared to pay high fees and take unknown risks.

**2006–2007** Arrivals of would-be immigrants from north Africa to Italy drop from 9,389 to 5,200 >>>  **2008** Although numbers of illegal immigrants making the crossing from north Africa are dropping, the crossing is more dangerous and the death rate remains high >>>

17

# Case Study: Diao Souncar Dieme, young man lost to the sea

Diao Souncar Dieme was in the news – and then briefly – only after his death. He was the only person to be positively identified from a group of young African men whose attempt to reach Europe had ended in disaster.

When 11 bodies were discovered in a sea-battered yacht off the small Caribbean island of Barbados in April 2006, it was a big story for the local *Daily News*. Reporter Tim Slinger followed the story over several months. He told readers of the mystery surrounding the bodies and of the international search to identify them and discover what had happened.

The story gained publicity in Spain and Portugal, home to many African immigrants. People who feared that their relatives and friends were among the dead got in touch with local newspapers and the Barbados authorities.

Slowly, they helped to put together a fuller story. The yacht had left Cape Verde islands, on Christmas Day 2005, carrying 50 young men from Guinea Bissau, Gambia and Senegal. Each had paid around 1,300 euros to be taken to Spain's Canary Islands. When the motor failed, the yacht was towed by another boat. Later, the towline was cut and the yacht drifted westward into the Atlantic, where most passengers were lost overboard. The remaining 11 died of dehydration and starvation on the boat.

Diao Souncar Dieme was identified because he had left a short note. 'I am from Senegal but have been living in Cape Verde for a year. Things are bad. I don't think that I will come out of this alive. Please send my family in Senegal some money.'

*Police and forensic experts inspect the `ghost ship' in the harbour at Bridgetown, Barbados, on 1 May 2006. Eleven bodies were found in the cramped cabin.*

**25 December 2005** Yacht leaves Cape Verde heading for Canary Islands >>>

**29 April 2006** Fishermen discover yacht off coast of Barbados with 11 bodies on board >>>

# WHAT THE WORLD THINKS...

These are four different articles commenting on Diao Souncar Dieme and the boat discovered off the Barbados coast in 2006. Compare and contrast the various viewpoints and see if you can find any more newspaper reports or other media discussing him or the ghost ship.

**El Pais, 20 May 2006**

## 21 BOAT DEATHS NAMED

*El Pais* is a national newspaper in Spain.

**Tim Slinger, 'Floating grave', Daily News, 1 May 2006**

*'Police forensic experts were last night trying to determine how 11 people, believed to come from an African country, perished at sea.'*

*Daily News* is a newspaper in Barbados.

**Guardian, 29 May 2006**

'After four months at sea, ghost ship with 11 petrified bodies washes up in Barbados – Letter left by dying man gives clue to investigators – Dozens of others thought to have perished en route'

**Tim Slinger, 'One of 11 dead Africans identified', Daily News, 24 August 2006**

*'A 29-year-old Senegalese man has been positively identified as one of 11 bodies discovered on a small yacht off Barbados four months ago. The identification of Diao Souncar Dieme followed forensic investigations, including DNA testing conducted by specialist Interpol teams locally and in the West African nation from which it is believed most of the deceased originated.'*

*Daily News* is a newspaper in Barbados.

 **15 January 2007** Body of Diao Souncar Dieme flown to Senegal for burial >>> **30 January 2007** Ten unidentified bodies buried in Barbados with Catholic and Muslim ceremonies >>>

**19**

# Chapter 4

# Cheap Labour – the Hidden Economy

In many countries, there are two economies. By far, the largest is the legitimate economy – the normal world of work and wages, taxes and social security. This is the world where most people live. Workers have legal rights, for example, to a minimum wage, to paid holidays and to join a trade union. They are free to leave their job and to compensation if they lose their job.

Then there is another world – the hidden or 'black' economy – where workers have no rights. Their wages are low, and sometimes paid late or not paid at all. They are charged high prices for food and accommodation. Neither they nor their employer pay taxes. The worker can be sacked without notice or compensation.

Many of the workers in the hidden economy have been trafficked. Some pay people smugglers to bring them across international borders. Once they have arrived, they contact friends or relatives who help with work and housing. They have little or no further contact with their traffickers. But others cannot escape – their lives, earnings and even their bodies belong to their traffickers.

*Migrant workers from Mexico picking strawberries in California. The farming industry in the state is largely dependent on migrant labour.*

*The Philippines trains many more nurses than it needs and many seek employment abroad, where salaries are higher and they can save money to support their families at home.*

## Overseas migration

For many would-be migrants, working abroad is a golden opportunity to earn money and improve their lives. In the rich West, even in a low-paid insecure job, they can earn much more than they could at home, where jobs are hard to come by and pay little. For example, in Senegal in west Africa, in 2006 the average income per person was US$670 a year, compared with US$30,000 in France. In Nicaragua, in central America, it was US$790 a year, compared with over US$41,400 in the USA.

In many countries, overseas migration is common. Millions of people from India, Pakistan and Bangladesh work in the oil-rich states of the Middle East. Women from the Philippines are recruited as nurses or maids in dozens of countries. These are examples of legal migration. Although workers may stay abroad for many years, they return on a regular basis and send money back home.

Legal immigration to rich Western countries is nearly always restricted to skilled workers or certain jobs, although some countries accept refugees or family members on a quota basis. But people still want to come and so patterns of illegal immigration have developed in many areas. For example, immigrants from Mexico and central America migrate northwards to the USA and people from the former Soviet Union migrate westwards to western Europe. Human traffickers and people smugglers enable them to travel and work – but the price people pay is a high one.

## How trafficking works

Traffickers offer people the opportunity to cross borders and achieve their dream of working and earning. Sometimes they claim that the jobs are legal with visas or work permits, but in many cases people know that they will be working in the black economy. The would-be migrants know that this is the case and are willing to take the risks involved.

Traffickers demand large sums of money to cover the costs of travel, food, accommodation, false papers and bribes for officials. Migrants sell land and borrow from family and moneylenders to finance their journey, which they will repay out of their future earnings. Often the traffickers act as moneylenders, charging

high rates of interest. If the migrant dies en route or in their new country, the family they leave behind is still responsible for paying the debt.

Not all trafficking involves international borders. In India, young boys are trafficked for work in carpet factories, while teenage girls go into the brothels of the big cities. Often the person who recruits them is seen as a trusted community member. The parents may believe that their child is going to a proper job, but in some cases they know what lies ahead. In other cases, no consent is involved and children are simply abducted.

*Rescued from the seas off Sicily, these would-be immigrants from Eritrea have attempted the Mediterranean crossing from Libya to Italy.*

**QUOTE >**

'To target the human trafficking industry you would have to have identification of traffickers in order to investigate the trafficking in persons cases, and prosecute and convict offenders. Unfortunately, very few cases are prosecuted successfully, resulting in a very small number of convictions.'

'Trafficking in Persons: Global Patterns' report, UNDOC, 2006.

*A young boy works in a carpet factory in India. These boys may have been sold by their parents or a 'trusted friend', or kidnapped by a gang.*

## Trapped workers

Trafficking is about fraud and deceit. The jobs offered either do not exist or are not as described. For example, a man may be promised a factory job, but find himself working in labouring or agriculture. The promised accommodation may mean sharing a dirty room with a dozen others. A young woman may be told that she will work as a waitress but find herself imprisoned in a locked room and forced into selling her body for sex. Because the trafficking gangs have complete control, their role is akin to a slave owner.

Why do trafficked workers stay in such conditions? The workers are in a strange environment, where they do not know the language or local people. They fear being thrown in jail or deported. If they try to leave, they are bullied and beaten. They are told that they must repay huge debts. It is not just the worker who is affected. The gangs threaten family members back home. Some workers may not want to return home, especially if they feel they have failed their family or will place them in danger.

## Trafficking gangs

Trafficking gangs are part of a long chain of crime. Gangs recruit would-be migrants in their home countries, promising them good jobs. They lend money to the migrants and their families, placing them in debt. They arrange transport, work and accommodation. They control the migrants once they arrive, and often take their passports and any money they have earned. They may use the workers in their own enterprises or rent them out to others. Finally, they may be involved in money laundering, to disguise the proceeds of their crimes.

Gangs can build complex networks across borders. For example, when UNDOC worked with the Italian authorities to track human trafficking victims from the Philippines to Italy, they found a criminal network which included gangs from the Philippines, Pakistan and Slovenia.

The victims were young women who were promised good jobs in Europe by so-called 'employment agencies'. The agencies arranged for the women to be flown from Manila to Bangkok, where they obtained Hungarian visas, and were flown on to Budapest in Hungary. They were then transported by road to Slovenia where smaller groups were smuggled into Italy by van or on foot. There they were delivered to a Filipino gang and taken to their final destination.

When journalist Misha Glenny investigated international crime, he uncovered a complex web of criminal networks. Criminal gangs came from many countries but particularly flourished in areas of conflict and social upheaval, such as Eastern Europe and the former Soviet Union. Gangs were often involved in smuggling drugs and weapons as well as people. Misha Glenny traced the journey of a young woman called Ludmilla from a lawless area called Transnistria, part of the former Soviet Union. Ludmilla was kidnapped by a gang and smuggled via Moscow to Israel, where she was sold to a brothel. When she finally escaped, she was deported as an illegal immigrant and left destitute.

## In the grip of the snakeheads

In the Fujian province in southern China, overseas migration has been going on for generations. People are driven by the belief that they can earn more and can better themselves. For some people the dream comes true; with their earnings

> **QUOTE >**
>
> 'Wife. Europe is a devilish prison. It is very hard to make a living here. To earn money, I have to endure the depths of bitterness. In this boring Europe I miss you and mother and our relatives very much.'
>
> **Lin Guoguang**, one of 21 Chinese immigrant workers who died in Morecambe Bay.

they build a large house and send their children to college.

Today, migrants are aided by criminal gangs known as 'snakeheads'. Families borrow money to pay the snakeheads to smuggle people to Europe or the USA for work. Once they reach their destination, they find themselves trapped. As illegal immigrants, they work in the black economy for low wages and without legal protection. Most do not speak English so are dependent on Chinese employers and

*A winter's night at Morecombe Bay in February 2004 saw the deaths of 23 Chinese cockle pickers in the freezing waters. Only 21 bodies were recovered, with 14 people rescued.*

gangmasters. It is easy for employers to cheat them or withhold wages. The workers live in fear that they will be discovered and deported before they have repaid their debts. But when things go wrong, as they did in Morecambe Bay in 2004 (see pages 26–27), then the families are left with huge debts.

# Case Study: Lin Liang Ren, convicted trafficker in Morecambe Bay case

*Lin Liang Ren, the gangmaster who sent dozens of people to work in dangerous conditions and then left them to die.*

In March 2006, Lin Liang Ren made the news when he was sentenced to 14 years imprisonment for manslaughter. But this was no ordinary trial. It received worldwide publicity, including in Lin's home country of China. The British media followed events closely, even devoting special programmes to the case.

Two years before, on the evening of 5 February 2004, emergency services were called to rescue people stranded in the waters of Morecambe Bay, in north-west England. The bay was well known for its complex currents and fast-advancing tides.

It was also known for its cockles, seafood which command high prices in international markets.

Dozens of people were harvesting cockles on that winter evening. All of them were inexperienced and untrained illegal immigrants from the Chinese province of Fujian. As the tides advanced, some made desperate calls on their mobiles to their families in China: 'We are going to die here'. 21 bodies were recovered from the waters, 14 people were rescued.

Lin Liang Ren was supervising the workers from the warmth of his car. Unlike them, he was educated and had arrived in Britain legally on a student visa. He didn't study but set himself up as a boss, a gangmaster, forging false papers for his illegal workers.

After he was arrested, he warned the survivors that there would be 'harmful consequences' for their families if they gave evidence against him. Far away in Fujian, there were assaults and threats against the bereaved families, now saddled with heavy debts.

Detective Superintendent Mick Gradwell said that there were probably links between the gangs in China and the gangs in England, 'The thread that runs through all of this is money.'

# WHAT THE WORLD THINKS...

These are three different news stories commenting on Lin Liang Ren and the Morecambe Bay cockle pickers. Compare and contrast the various viewpoints and see if you can find any more newspaper reports or other media discussing him and the trafficked victims.

**'Lin Liang Ren's career of exploitation', Press Association, 4 March 2006**

'A heavy gambler with suspected links to China's so-called Snakeshead people-smuggling gangs, gangmaster Lin Liang Ren was at the centre of a conspiracy that led to 23 deaths.

Unlike many of those people, Lin was fleeing neither persecution nor poverty. "He was someone of substance in China", said Detective Superintendent Mick Gradwell, who lead the inquiry.'

**'Press anger at "Devil's beach" tragedy', BBC News website, 11 February 2004**

'The deaths of 19 cockle pickers have prompted front-page coverage of the tragedy at Britain's Morecambe Bay, dubbed "the Devil's beach" in the Chinese media.

Editorials warned migrants against seeking dangerous and illegal work abroad, while some papers tracked down victims' and survivors' families.'

**'Granada wins Bafta for Morecambe Bay trial coverage', Press Gazette, 21 May 2007**

'ITV's coverage of the Morecambe Bay cockling trial has been awarded a Bafta. The broadcaster's regional news programme in the North-West, Granada Reports picked up the award for best news coverage at last night's ceremony.

Granada had followed the long-running manslaughter trial at Preston Crown Court after some 21 Chinese illegal immigrants were swept away to their death by tides while collecting cockles in Morecambe Bay, Lancashire, in 2004.'

# Chapter 5

# Servant Slaves – Trapped in the Home

Some of the world's most exploited people are almost entirely hidden from public view and are rarely featured in the media. These are domestic servants.

A century ago, there were vast numbers of domestic servants in Europe and North America. Living in overcrowded attic rooms, they carried out the backbreaking tasks of cleaning, cooking and caring in an era when labour costs were low and labour-saving devices were in their infancy.

Today, this sort of domestic service is much less common in Western countries, although it is still widespread in poorer countries where labour is cheap and unemployment is high. Often, the servants are young children or teenagers who work long hours for little or no pay. The largest numbers are found in south and south-east Asia, in Africa and Latin America.

> ### QUOTE >
>
> 'The man's name was Jean. He gave my father 500 francs [50 pence] and my brothers 500 to share. I had never met Jean before.'
>
> **Victoria**, 9-year-old girl, rescued while being transported to Gabon as a domestic servant in 2001.

## Trafficking in west Africa

The United Nations Children's Fund (UNICEF) says that there are clear links between children in domestic service and human trafficking, within and between countries. One trafficking route that has gained media attention is the trafficking of young girls for domestic service in west Africa. There have been many reports of girls from Benin and Togo being trafficked to Gabon in dangerous, overcrowded ships.

In Benin, it is common to send village children to live with relatives in the city and this has proved to be an adept cover for traffickers to buy and sell children. Traffickers often pose as family friends who will find the child a place with a good family and give the parents a small amount for their help. The practice is known as 'trafic-ouvier'. When children are sold outright, it is called `trafic-verite'.

While some parents are happy to sell their child for money, most parents genuinely believe that they are doing the right thing and giving their child an opportunity to learn new skills, perhaps even gain an education. More recently, this abuse has been the target of campaigns by governments, charitable groups and non-government organisations while the news media has highlighted some prominent cases.

But it is not just in the developing world that people are trafficked into domestic

*Two young girls who are victims of trafficking at a safe house in Cotonou, the capital of Benin. They are the lucky ones. Many thousands are trafficked into domestic slavery at home or abroad.*

slavery. There have been cases reported of women and children being trafficked into Western countries. Often they are promised a good job, with an opportunity to send earnings back home. Once they arrive, they find themselves locked in a strange house, working long hours cleaning, cooking and looking after children. Escape is almost impossible.

They may not speak the local language and often the employer takes their passport. Although this is illegal, it continues as a hidden practice.

# Case Study: Hector Rodriguez, rescuer of modern-day slaves

Kumari Sabbithi, Jaoquina Quadros and Tina Fernandes owe their freedom to Hector Rodriguez. If he hadn't helped them, they would have remained in domestic slavery.

However, their ordeal didn't take place in India or Latin America, but in the suburbs of Washington, as domestic servants for a Kuwaiti diplomat, Major Waleed Al-Saleh. The women saw the jobs as an opportunity to earn money to send to their families in India. But the reality was very different. The women were routinely beaten and mistreated. Their wages were tiny and they worked 18-hour days. They were trapped in the house and rarely allowed outside.

Hector Rodriquez lived nearby. `I was washing my car and one of them was pacing up and down the street, right in front of my driveway, looking at me with the fear of God in her face.' He crossed the street and asked her if she was in danger. She told him of their conditions. Later, she told her co-workers of the encounter.

Some time later, Mr Rodriquez heard a loud knocking on his door. It was Kumari Sabbithi, shivering in the bitter cold. She had escaped after a beating. Mr Rodriquez called the police, and later helped the other two women.

The US authorities said that they should be treated as victims of trafficking and allowed to stay in the USA. However, because Major Al-Saleh was a diplomat, it was unlikely that he would be prosecuted.

Only a few media accounts mentioned Hector Rodriquez and his humane action in rescuing the women. He is still appalled and says, 'How is it possible that – in the country where freedom is relished – these atrocities are allowed to happen under the umbrella of diplomatic immunity?'

The American Civil Liberties Union (ACLU) took up the cause of the three women. They began a lawsuit charging the diplomat, his wife and the government of Kuwait with trafficking the women and forcing them to work in slavery-like conditions. ACLU said the Kuwait government should have known of the problem with the diplomat and acted to prevent it.

In September 2007, Major Al-Saleh and his family left the USA rather than face prosecution without diplomatic immunity. In November, the US government forced the diplomat to resign his job at the Kuwait embassy and banned both the diplomat and his wife from ever returning to the USA. The government said that it would investigate other cases of diplomatic abuse.

| **August 2005** Kumari Sabbithi first approaches Hector Rodriguez >>> | **October 2005** Sabbithi flees Major Al-Saleh's house and seeks shelter with Rodriguez >>> | **January 2007** American Civil Liberties Union begins lawsuit >>> |

# WHAT THE WORLD THINKS...

These are three different publications commenting on
Hector Rodriguez and his rescue of the three domestic slaves.
Compare and contrast the various viewpoints and see if you
can find any more newspaper reports or other media
discussing any other cases of modern-day slavery.

Frank Langfitt, 'Servants: Diplomat Held Us as
Suburban Slaves', *National Public Radio* website,
1 March 2007

'Three former servants are suing a Kuwaiti diplomat,
alleging that he treated them like slaves in his suburban
home in Washington, D.C. The workers are poor women from
India, and they say the diplomat worked them for more than
15 hours a day. They also claim his wife beat one of them
repeatedly…But even if the women can to prove their
charges, they will have a difficult time winning their case:
The Kuwaitis deny the accusations and say they have
diplomatic immunity.'

Frank Langfitt,
*National Public Radio*
website,
1 March 2007

'Hector Rodriguez took
in Kumari Sabbithi the
night she ran away. Later,
two other domestic
workers from the house
sought refuge with him.'

Henri E. Cauvin,
'Workers Allege Abuse by Kuwaiti
Attache', *Washington Post*,
18 January 2007

'Three Indian women who worked in the
McLean home of a Kuwaiti military
attache filed a lawsuit yesterday alleging
that they were brought to the United
States illegally and abused and exploited
by the diplomat and his wife.'

**September 2007**
Major Al-Saleh and
family leave USA >>>

**November 2007** Major
Al-Saleh and his wife are
banned from USA >>>

# Chapter 6

# Bodies for Sale – Trafficking for Sex

All over the world, girls and young women are bought and sold for sex. UNDOC says that 80 per cent of recorded victims of trafficking are women and girls who are forced into sex work. About half of the victims are under 18 years of age.

The most numerous cases occur in poor developing countries, especially in south and south-east Asia. Some trafficking happens both within countries and across borders. For example, every year thousands of young girls are trafficked from Nepal and the foothills of the Indian Himalayas to the brothels of Kolkota (formerly Calcutta) and Mumbai (formerly Bombay). A similar trade takes place in Thailand, as girls from the poor north-east and the even poorer countries of Cambodia and Laos end up in the booming sex industry of Bangkok.

Families sometimes knowingly sell their children to traffickers, but often they are

*A young woman waits for customers at a brothel in India. Every year thousands of women and girls from India and Nepal are sold to brothels by traffickers.*

> **QUOTE >**
>
> 'The most horrific aspect is the trafficking of young girls. We met a young Lithuanian who found that even before she'd arrived in this "land of opportunity", she'd been sold on. She was eventually sold seven times. She only escaped after the man who'd bought her for just £1,500 took her to a nightclub to show her off – several English girls distracted him while she escaped to run to a police station, but he'd already raped her four times.'
>
> **Rageh Omar**, journalist on his new television series *Crime Invasion*, *Daily Telegraph*, 4 October 2007.

 **The United Nations Office on Drugs and Crime (UNODC) reports:** >>> | 77% of victims of trafficking are women >>> | There are four times the number of girls who are victims of trafficking than boys >>>

*This art installation by the Helen Bamber Foundation, on display in Trafalgar Square, London, in 2007, illustrates the plight of women involved in sex trafficking from Eastern Europe to the UK. Transport carriers typically used for trafficking were used for the exhibition.*

deceived into thinking that their child will be going to a good job. It's not just a matter of poverty but of gender. Girls are not valued as highly as boys, who are more likely to be sent to school and remain with their family.

More recently, trafficking networks have developed bringing young women and girls from Eastern Europe and the former Soviet Union (USSR) into western Europe. Once again, the major push is poverty and unemployment, but also abuse and neglect. Traffickers focus on recruiting uneducated teenagers from poor families, who know little of the outside world. The promise of a `good job' in a rich country is a tempting prospect, but the reality is very different.

After a long, uncomfortable journey, a girl will find herself imprisoned in a dingy room in an unknown city. She is usually raped and beaten and told that she must sell her body to pay off her debts (which she may not even realise she has accumulated). She finds herself unable to escape and or even to communicate if she doesn't know the language. She may be moved around and sold to another gang. She may not even know the name of the city where she is held. A few escape or are rescued in police raids on brothels, but most girls are trapped.

**87% of the trafficking reported involves sexual exploitation >>>**

# Case Study: The anonymous woman, sold into slavery by people traffickers

Media stories on sex trafficking often focus on sensational aspects, such as police raids and criminal trials, but the victims rarely get the opportunity to tell how they came to be trafficked or what happened after they were rescued.

The reasons are straightforward. Most victims are young women who are traumatised by their experiences of being imprisoned, beaten and raped. Many say they are ashamed and do not want their families to know what happened to them, especially if they return home ill and penniless. They are in a foreign country, in many cases illegally, and fear they will be deported back to their home country. They are also frightened that their traffickers will track them down and punish them and their families.

For this reason, when women and girls do tell their stories, it is nearly always anonymously or speaking under a pseudonym. But often the images used to illustrate their story are misleading, distracting or glamorise their situation. They present the victim as the stereotype of a sexy, young woman rather than a frightened, brutalised human being.

For the women and girls who are rescued, the future is uncertain. Many are returned to their home countries and reunited with their families. Sometimes this works well but many are rejected and find themselves alone without jobs or money. Some even find themselves falling into the hands of traffickers yet again.

*Traffickers deliberately target vulnerable young girls in poor families. They are sold into the sex trade and find themselves beaten and trapped in brothels.*

# WHAT THE WORLD THINKS...

These are three different publications commenting on sex trafficking. Compare and contrast the various viewpoints and see if you can find any more newspaper reports or other media discussing this form of human trafficking.

**'3 in court after sauna raid',**
*The Sun* **website,**
**1 October 2005**

'Three people accused of running a brothel where 19 women were found during a police raid appeared in court yesterday. The women, mostly from eastern Europe or the Far East, were found in the Cuddles sauna in Birmingham on Thursday night.'

**'Sex slave regrets "ruined" life',**
*BBC News* **website,**
**19 March 2007**

'Beaten, betrayed and forced to have sex with up to 20 men a day – it sounds like a horror story but this is the testimony of a sex slave in Leicester.
Edita, who was 19 when she was brought into the UK illegally from Lithuania, said her life had been ruined by the experience.
The Home Office estimates 4,000 women are trafficked into the UK every year.'

**'Art for humanity's sake reveals sex trade horror',**
*Evening Standard*
**24 September 2007**

'Long queues greeted the launch of the latest artwork to take up residence in Trafalgar Square – seven transport containers illustrating the suffering of women trafficked as sex slaves.
The crates are the kind used to smuggle people into Britain, but have been painted with images designed to shock the viewer into awareness of the realities of the sex trade.'

# Chapter 7

# Responses to Human Trafficking

## Action to stop trafficking

Trafficking is big business, yet what is being done to stop it? In most countries, it is not a high-profile issue and it still gets little attention from the government, law enforcement agencies or the media.

Often the lead is taken by non-government organisations (NGOs), campaigning groups and charities. It is these groups who investigate the situation and, where possible, make contact with victims, help them to escape and rebuild their lives. Some groups have brought law suits to support victims. Others have launched awareness campaigns to inform and educate potential victims so they are less likely to fall prey to traffickers.

Governments have tended to lag behind on human trafficking, even where there are strong laws against it. Few traffickers are caught, prosecuted and punished.

*Campaigning against the sex trade. Women from the Coalition Against Trafficking of Women (CATW) at a press conference after a meeting of women activists in Asia.*

| UNODC reports few prosecutions and convictions of traffickers: >>> | 2003 Lithuania – 20 prosecuted, 8 convicted >>> | 2003 Netherlands – 117 prosecuted, 106 convicted >>> | 2004 USA – 59 prosecuted, 43 convicted >>> |
|---|---|---|---|

There is little public pressure for governments to act – trafficking is a hidden problem whose victims are largely invisible. But as police forces realise the size of the problem, many are giving it higher priority and increased funding.

## International action

Trafficking has long been recognised as a crime and a violation of human rights by the UN and other international bodies. Some of the earliest international documents were concerned with forced labour and trafficking in women and children. However, the focus was largely on governments upholding human rights, rather than acting against traffickers.

In 2000, the UN adopted a new Convention Against Transnational Organised Crime, known as the Palermo Convention. The Convention came into force in 2003 and is divided into two protocols – the first dealing with human trafficking and the second with people smuggling. The Palermo Convention defines trafficking, and outlines legal and law enforcement measures to prevent and combat trafficking and punish the traffickers, and to protect and assist the victims of trafficking. It also urges countries to co-operate with each other, in order to tackle trafficking across borders. By May 2008, 117 governments had signed the protocol on trafficking, committing themselves to take action.

The Palermo Convention is overseen by UNDOC. In March 2007, UNDOC

> ### QUOTE >
>
> 'The good news about modern slavery is that, possibly for the first time in human history, it can be eradicated. With laws against it in every country, and the lack of any large vested economic interest supporting it, slavery can be ended when the public and governments make it a priority.'
>
> **Kevin Bales**, 'Of human bondage', *Financial Times*, 15 March 2007.

launched a new campaign, the Global Initiative to Fight Human Trafficking (GIFT), to raise awareness of trafficking worldwide, including informing potential victims of the dangers of trafficking and reducing the demand for services and products that rely on slave labour.

However, critics point out that despite the Palermo Convention and well-intentioned campaigns like GIFT, human trafficking is likely to continue in one form or another as long as it remains a hugely profitable enterprise. To end trafficking, governments, police forces and legal systems will have to co-operate effectively across borders to overcome the criminal networks that organise the trafficking routes and control the vulnerable and frightened victims.

## Tackling the causes of trafficking

Many campaigners say international conventions and strong laws, however well applied, will not stop trafficking. Rather, they point to the need to tackle the causes of trafficking that affect the supply of trafficked people and the demand for their services.

*In many countries, girls are regarded as being of lesser value than boys and are more likely to be abandoned in orphanages, like these baby girls in Korea, or sold to traffickers.*

Poverty is a major cause. Victims come from the poorest countries and are trafficked to richer areas, within their country or aboard. Some go willingly, others are coerced or abducted. Many know the risks but feel that it is the only way they can escape poverty. Campaigners say that rich countries must act to help poor countries overcome the poverty gap.

Some campaigners go further and say that the best way to stop international trafficking and people smuggling is for rich countries to reform their immigration systems, so people from poor countries can live and work there legally, on a temporary or permanent basis.

However, trafficking is not just about poverty, but neglect, abuse and discrimination. Traffickers know how to target the most vulnerable people, such as orphans and uneducated young girls. As long as some societies regard girls as of less value than boys, families will sign them over to traffickers. Making sure all children have an education, and that girls are treated equally to boys, are important weapons in the fight against trafficking.

Supporting and rehabilitating victims is vital. All too often, those who are rescued and returned home, find themselves shunned by their family – some are even returned to the traffickers.

But the demand side of trafficking is also important. Would we buy goods or services produced by trafficked people? Most of us would say no, but others are not so worried.

*Child camel jockeys racing in 1987. The use of child jockeys is now illegal in many Gulf states, but many people suspect it continues outside the law.*

## Yet trafficking continues

Despite government and international efforts, trafficking continues, often in surprising and unusual ways. Trafficking is not just a big business, but a flexible business which adapts to new opportunities. When laws change, traffickers find new ways to operate.

For example, take the situation in the Gulf States: camel racing is very popular and young boys are sought as jockeys. Most come from poor countries, especially Pakistan, Bangladesh and Sudan. Some children are sold by their families, others are kidnapped by criminals. Being a camel jockey is a terrifying experience and children are regularly injured or even killed while racing.

The United Arab Emirates (UAE) has passed several anti-trafficking laws. However, the use of boy jockeys continues. In 2005, the UAE government announced that child jockeys would be replaced by specially constructed robots and that the boys would be returned to their home countries and given care, education and compensation. Whether this is really a solution remains to be seen. Campaigners and the media should keep a close watch.

**July 2005** UAE outlaws child camel jockeys, and starts process of sending them home >>>

**September 2006** US law firm files lawsuit against government of Dubai for continuing to use child camel jockeys >>>

# Case Study: Yayi Bayam Diouf, anti-trafficker campaigner

Yayi Bayam Diouf is a village woman from Senegal, yet she has spoken at international meetings and been interviewed by journalists from all over the world. She is the founder of an organisation called Association des femmes pour la lutte contre l'émigration clandestine (Women's association for the struggle against clandestine migration).

*Yayi Bayam Diouf, campaigner against dangerous and illegal migration, at a meeting in Thiaroye, Senegal, in 2006.*

The organisation urges young men not to fall victim to the people smugglers who tempt them to travel to Europe via Spain's Canary Islands. The journey is a dangerous one, in rusty, overcrowded boats. Many men are drowned at sea, while many of those who do make it are sent back to Senegal.

Madame Diouf's campaign arose from personal experience. Her only son died at sea, together with 81 other young men from her village. She had contributed to the funds for his voyage. She decided to turn her bitterness and grief into an attempt to stop similar tragedies.

Madame Diouf says poverty is the main reason for the migration. Their small fishing boats cannot compete with massive European fishing trawlers, and fish stocks have declined dramatically. Now local fishermen are unemployed. No wonder they want to go to Europe.

Although it lacks resources, the campaign is now making an impact and it seems that numbers of migrants are starting to drop. Meanwhile, the Spanish government is airing advertisements on the dangers of people smuggling. But, says Madame Diouf, unless the problems of poverty are solved, young people face a bleak future in Senegal.

# WHAT THE WORLD THINKS...

These are three different publications commenting on Yayi Bayam Diouf and her efforts. Compare and contrast the various viewpoints and see if you can find any more newspaper reports or other media discussing human trafficking in Senegal.

**Jean Philippe Chauzy, 'Mother Courage fights irregular migration in Senegal', *Migration*, November 2006**

'Every week the association holds meetings with the young men of Thiaroye to try and persuade them not to emigrate clandestinely. "I tell them that out of 100 men who have left, 50 have died at sea, 25 haven't given news of their whereabouts for more than nine months, ten have been sent back from Spain and the rest are probably in camps or have made it to Spain where they are without a proper job. So in the end, it is better to stay here", says Yayi.'

**'Mother's battle against Senegal migration', *BBC News*, Dakar, 6 November 2006**

'Yayi Bayam Diouf says that for the past two months she has managed to prevent any boats leaving her home area in Senegal, loaded with migrants trying to reach Spain's Canary Islands – making her campaign more effective than all the warships and planes sent to the Atlantic Ocean by the European Union.'

**'Spain begins anti-migration ads', *BBC News 24*, 20 September 2007**

'The Spanish government has begun airing emotional television adverts across West Africa as part of its attempts to combat illegal immigration.

The [US]$1.4m media campaign is to run for six weeks and has begun in Senegal. The aim is to discourage potential migrants from attempting the dangerous 12-day voyage by boat to the Canary Islands.'

# Chapter 8

# Human Trafficking and the Media

How does the media cover the issue of human trafficking? Given the scale of the problem affecting almost every country in the world, you would expect it to feature regularly in the press and on television bulletins. However, this is very far from being the case.

In fact, there is very little media attention on human trafficking, especially compared with other criminal activities, such as gun crime, drugs or money laundering – even though the gangs involved in human trafficking are likely also to be involved in these activities. Even books and films rarely feature human trafficking. As a subject, it is seen as less glamorous or exciting than illegal gambling, robbery or gun-running.

Where there are news or features on human trafficking, they tend to focus on certain types of trafficking, such as people smuggling, illegal immigrants and the sex trade, rather than domestic slaves or traditional slavery.

Sometimes trafficking does make news headlines, usually when people die in large numbers or in unusual situations.

*Ai Qin Lin, one of the leading actors in* Ghosts, *a 2006 film which tells the story of the Morecombe Bay cockle pickers (see pages 26–27), one of the few films to focus on human trafficking.*

*The news story of the rescue efforts for the Morecambe Bay cockle pickers made the front page in* The Times *on 6 February 2004.*

# Race to save cockle-pickers from drowning in bay

**By Ellen Connolly**

FIFTEEN people believed to have been picking cockles were at risk of drowning last night after becoming trapped by a strong tide in Morecambe Bay, Lancashire. A further eight were rescued.

The group was believed to be Chinese and had been alerted to the danger of collecting cockles in the area, which is notorious for quicksand and strong, unexpected tidal flows.

"The tide went fairly rapidly from waist level on these people up to their necks," said Rick Phillips, from RAF Kinloss, which was involved in the rescue operation.

Four people were taken to hospital suffering from hypothermia, and another four were found on the shore. They were being questioned last night by Lancashire police. Peter Lovett-Horn, a police spokesman, said that the search would continue overnight. "Our biggest problem is that these people don't want to be found, largely because they are probably illegal immigrants," he said. "Bit by bit

we're getting news that they have been seen wandering around the shore."

The men were collecting cockles 1½ miles from the shore when they became trapped on a sandbank, an MoD spokeswoman said. The emergency call was received at 9.10pm. Two RAF search and rescue helicopters were at the scene at Hest Bank.

The operation was co-ordinated by Liverpool Coastguard. Morecambe lifeboat, a hovercraft, the Fleetwood lifeboat, two RAF helicopters and a police helicopter were involved. The stranded group did not speak English, which added to the difficulties.

Last August police arrested 37 Chinese people who were picking cockles without a licence in the area.

For example, in June 2000, the bodies of 58 Chinese people were discovered in a locked lorry at the English port of Dover. The two survivors described how they were trapped in darkness as temperatures soared. A Dutch truck driver was convicted of manslaughter and conspiracy to smuggle immigrants, and was sentenced to 14 years' jail.

## The real story?

What role does the media play in exposing human trafficking? With a few exceptions, their role is minor compared with that of campaigning groups and charities. Some media people contend the role of the media is to investigate and report the news, rather than lead campaigns. But newspapers will often take up a particular cause, report extensively on it and use their editorial pages to demand government action or a change in the law.

Not surprisingly, victims of trafficking rarely have an opportunity to present their story. Even if they escape, few have access to the media. They are traumatised, frightened and fear they will be deported. And some, especially young children, simply don't understand what has happened to them. Without a human face and a strong voice, media interest is limited. For the moment, human trafficking remains a rarely-told story.

**QUOTE >**

'MTV, the most popular music channel in the Asia-Pacific region, will soon be playing a different tune. Soon MTV Thailand will have live and hip music giving way to the harrowing accounts of human trafficking victims. No glam shots and glitzy productions here, just raw and oftentimes shocking images that will make young MTV fans sit up. Trafficking will get a human face through the personal accounts of Anna, Eka and Min Aung.'

**Lynette Lee Corporal**, IPS Asia-Pacific, 2005.

# Case Study: Julia Ormond, Goodwill Ambassador for UNDOC

Julia Ormond is an actress who has starred in Hollywood blockbusters as well as small independent films. In 2005, she took on a new role as a UN Goodwill Ambassador for UNDOC, to help raise the profile of the issue of human trafficking.

She first learned about the issue in the 1990s from a friend, Gillian Caldwell of the Global Survivor Network, who co-ordinated a two-year, undercover investigation into the trafficking of women from Eastern Europe.

In her UN role, Julia Ormond visits projects to combat trafficking to learn

*Actor Julia Ormond talks with US Representative Christopher Smith (left) and State Department advisor on trafficking John Miller (right), at a House International Relations Committee hearing in Washington, USA, on 14 June 2006.*

about the reality of the situation. She uses her experiences when urging governments and international bodies to take action. In 2006, she spoke before the US Congress and, in 2007, she supported the launch of UNDOC's GIFT.

Julia Ormond has also recorded short radio spots to be aired on radio stations worldwide in order to raise awareness of trafficking and how it can be prevented. She says, 'It is very hard for victims of trafficking to tell their stories, so by meeting victims privately and sympathetically to hear their stories I hope to relay them on their behalf to the outside world...The difference between the drug trade and trafficking is that drugs can be sold only once but human beings can be sold over and over.'

# WHAT THE WORLD THINKS...

These are three different publications commenting on Julia Ormond's work on behalf of UNDOC. Compare and contrast the various viewpoints and see if you can find any more newspaper reports or other media discussing the Goodwill Ambassador and GIFT.

### USA Today, 26 March 2007

'Julia Ormond appealed to police agencies worldwide Monday to share information and resources in hopes of combating human trafficking.

The 42-year-old British actress, who co-starred with Harrison Ford in 1995's *Sabrina*, spoke in London to help publicize a new U.N. campaign to combat [the] 21st-century slave trade. The initiative came a day after the 200th anniversary of the passage of Britain's anti-slavery law.'

*USA Today* is an American daily national newspaper.

### 'House Committee Focuses on Human Trafficking', *Voice of America*, 15 June 2006

'A congressional subcommittee held a hearing Wednesday on the State Department's 2006 report on human trafficking around the world. British actress Julia Ormond, who is also a Goodwill Ambassador for the United Nations, told about meeting the victims of human trafficking in Ghana, India, Thailand and Cambodia.'

*Voice of America* is the official external radio and television service of the US federal government.

### 'An independent Voice from the United Nations', *Maxims News* website 23 July 2007

'Goodwill Ambassador and renowned actress Julia Ormond called for global efforts to combat human trafficking and called for international efforts to change the root causes of the problem in a press briefing at the U.N. on Thursday.'

**asylum** Protection given to people who have left their country because they were in danger.

**brothel** A place where commercial sex takes place, which may also be a living space for sex workers.

**CATW** The Coalition Against Trafficking in Women International is an NGO that was founded in 1988 that promotes women's human rights, particularly campaigning against sex trafficking of women and girls.

**CAST** The Coalition to Abolish Slavery and Trafficking, established in 1998, is a multi-ethnic human rights organisation assists people trafficked for the purpose of forced labour and slavery-like practices and works towards ending all instances of such human rights violations.

**clandestine** Done secretly.

**coercion** To compel someone by threats or force.

**compensation** A payment in return for a loss (e.g. of a job).

**convention** An international legal instrument, by which when signed and ratified (agreed) by a country, becomes legally binding (lawful).

**deception** To cause someone to believe something that is untrue.

**diplomat** Representative of a government based in another country.

**diplomatic immunity** Freedom from prosecution and conviction for crimes or other offences given to diplomats while representing their governments when abroad.

**elude** To escape or avoid.

**euro** The currency used in many European Union countries.

**exploitation** To work someone without proper pay or reward.

**fraud** Criminal deception or dishonesty.

**gender** Distinction between male and female, often refers to the lower status women and girls hold in society compared to men and boys.

**gangmaster** A person who organises groups of migrant labourers, legal or illegal, in the UK.

**GIFT** The Global Initiative to End Human Trafficking is the UN initiative launched in 2007 to raise international awareness of human trafficking.

**illegal** Unlawful.

**illegal immigrant** (see undocumented migrant)

**ILO** The International Labour Organisation is a UN body setting standards for workers and employers.

**immigrant** A person who travels to another country to live and work.

**immigration** The permanent move to another country.

**iniquitous** Very wrong.

**interest** Charge applied in return for borrowing money. Interest is usually a percentage of the money borrowed.

**legitmate** Lawful, above board.

**migrant** Someone who moves from one region of their country to another, or to another country.

**NGO** A non-government organisation is an independent, non-commercial organisation, for example, a charity or campaigning group.

**persecution** Treating people badly because of their ethnic group, culture, religious or political beliefs.

**prejudice** Negative feelings towards a group of people, which are not based on facts.

**prosecute** To put a person on trial for breaking the law.

**protocol** An additional document attached to a convention, which spells out in more detail an aspect of the convention.

**refugee** A person who flees their country because they are being persecuted or threatened by their government, because of their political view or because of their race, ethnic group, sexual orientation, etc.

**reparations** Making amends, usually through a money payment, e.g. to people who have been persecuted or enslaved, or to their descendents.

**snakehead** Chinese term for people smuggler; 'human snake' – people who are smuggled.

**slave** A person owned by another person, and whose time or labour is not their own. Slavery is now considered to be a violation of human rights.

**stereotype** A negative view about a whole group of people, which is not based on facts, for example, 'asylum seekers are scroungers'.

**Soviet Union (USSR)** A country consisting of Russia and a number of other East European, Baltic and Central Asian countries, which existed from 1922 to 1991.

**UN** The United Nations is an organisation founded at the end of World War II (1945), with the aim of preventing further wars and upholding human rights. Today it has 192 countries as members.

**UNDOC** The United Nations' Office on Drugs and Crime is an organisation establisheded in 1997 to fight against illicit drugs and international crime on an international level.

**undocumented migrant** A person who has not entered the country according to the immigration laws.

**UNICEF** The United Nations' Children's Fund is an organisation operating in 190 countries working to promote children's health, education and general wellbeing.

## FURTHER INFORMATION >

### BOOKS

*Child Labour,*
by Kaye Stearman (Heinemann, 2004)

*Disposable People: New Slavery in the Global Economy,*
by Kevin Bales (University of California Press, 2004)

*McMafia: Crime without Frontiers*
by Misha Glenny (Bodley Head, 2008)

*Slavery Today,*
by Kaye Stearman (Wayland, 1999)

### WEBSITES

Anti-Slavery International
**www.antislavery.org**
*The oldest international human rights organisation.*

Global Initiative to Fight Human Trafficking (GIFT)
**www.ungift.org**
*UN initiative.*

Coalition to Abolish Slavery and Trafficking (CAST)
**www.castla.org**
*US-based anti-slavery group.*

Coalition Against Trafficking in Women (CATW)
**www.catwinternational.org**
*Focuses on trafficking of women and girls.*

*Ghosts*
**www.ghosts.uk.com**
*Website of the Morecambe Victims Fund, linked to the film,* Ghosts.

Human Trafficking
**www.humantrafficking.org**
*Resources on trafficking.*

Not for Sale
**www.notforsalecampaign.org**
*US-based campaigning group.*

UK Human Trafficking Centre
**www.ukhtc.org**
*UK government agency.*

UN Office on Drugs and Crime
**www.undoc.org**
*Information on trafficking.*

US Department of State Office to Monitor and Combat Trafficking in Persons
**www.state.gov/g/tip/**
*Information on US efforts to tackle trafficking.*